EQ4
BLOCK BOOK

EQ4
BLOCK BOOK

ELECTRIC QUILT COMPANY
419 GOULD STREET SUITE 2
BOWLING GREEN OH 43402
WWW.ELECTRICQUILT.COM

Contents

1 Classic Pieced

1 Classic Pieced
Album (Autograph) Blocks

Album Block

Album - Variable Star

Album - Variable Star II

Album - Variable Star III

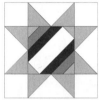

Album - Variable Star IV

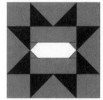

Album - Variable Star V

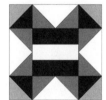

Album - Variable Star VI

Album - Variable Star VII

Album - V. Star VIII

Album - Variable Star IX

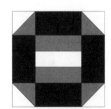

Album - Churn Dash Var.

Album Block II

Album Block III

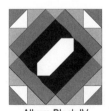

Album Block iV

Album Block V

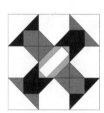

Album Block VI

Album Block VII

Album Block VIII

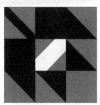

Leaf Album Block

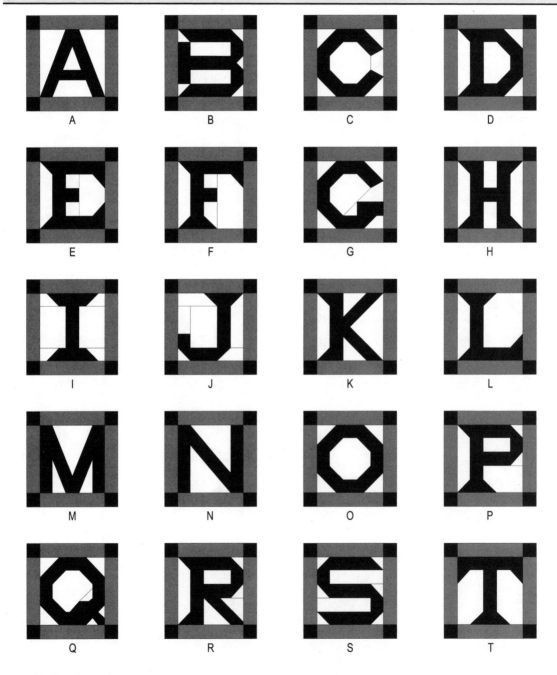

A

B

C

D

E

F

G

H

I

J

K

L

M

N

O

P

Q

R

S

T

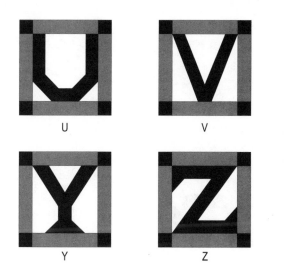

U   V   W   X

Y   Z

1 Classic Pieced Alphabet (Traditional)

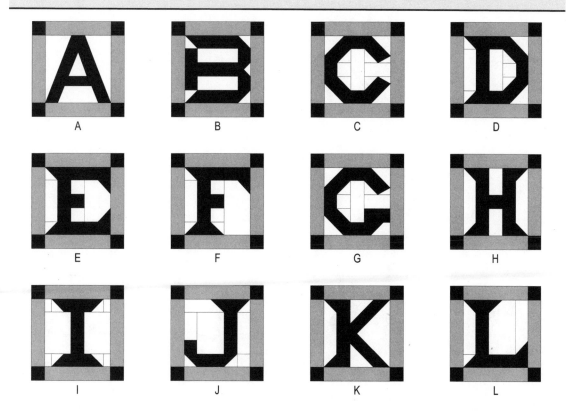

A   B   C   D

E   F   G   H

I   J   K   L

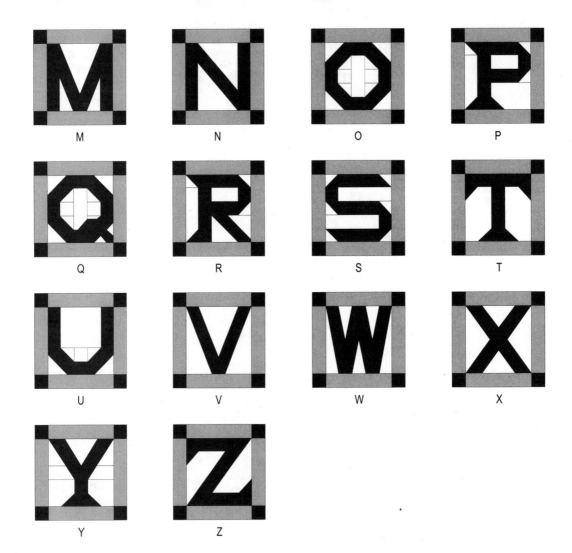

M   N   O   P

Q   R   S   T

U   V   W   X

Y   Z

1 Classic Pieced
Antique Mosaics

Mosaic, No. 1

Mosaic, No. 1(2)

Mosaic, No. 2

Mosaic, No. 2(2)

Mosaic, No. 3

Mosaic, No. 3(2)

Mosaic, No. 4

Mosaic, No. 4(2)

Mosaic, No. 5

Mosaic, No. 5(2)

Mosaic, No. 6

Mosaic, No. 10

Mosaic, No. 10(2)

Mosaic, No. 11

Mosaic, No. 13

Mosaic, No. 13(2)

Mosaic, No. 15

Mosaic, No. 17

Mosaic, No. 18

Mosaic, No. 18(2)

Mosaic, No. 19

Mosaic, No. 20

Mosaic, No. 21

Mosaic, No. 21(2)

Mosaic, No. 22

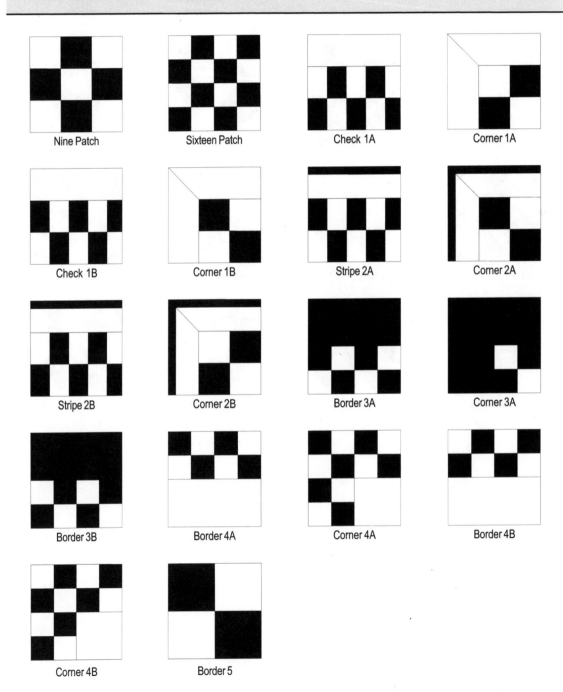

Nine Patch

Sixteen Patch

Check 1A

Corner 1A

Check 1B

Corner 1B

Stripe 2A

Corner 2A

Stripe 2B

Corner 2B

Border 3A

Corner 3A

Border 3B

Border 4A

Corner 4A

Border 4B

Corner 4B

Border 5

1 Classic Pieced
Classics

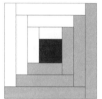

Log Cabin

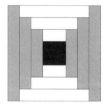

Log Cabin (2)

Ohio Star

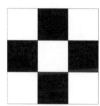

Nine Patch

Double Wedding Ring

Quarter Wedding Ring

Lady of the Lake

Flying Geese

Bow Tie

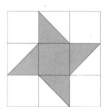

Friendship Star

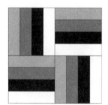

Rail Fence

Shoo Fly

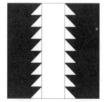

Tree Everlasting

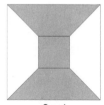

Spool

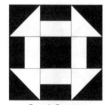

Greek Square

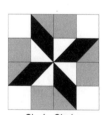

Clay's Choice

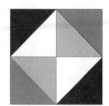

Broken Dishes

Birds in the Air

Attic Window

Old Maid's Puzzle

Whirlwind

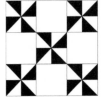

Pin Wheels

Corn and Beans

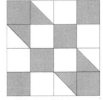

Road to Oklahoma

Cross and Crown

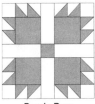

Bear's Paw

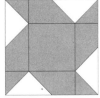

Churn Dash

Indian Hatchets

Wild Goose Chase

Monkey Wrench

1 Classic Pieced
Compass & Wheels

Compass Star

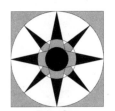

Daisy Star

Sunburst

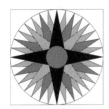

Chips and Whetstones

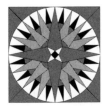

Mariner's Compass

Mariner's Compass

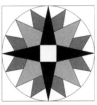

Star Wheel

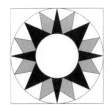

Circle Star

Pinwheel Circle

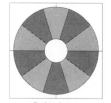

Baby Aster

Wheel of Chance

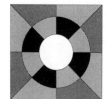

Transparent Circle

Jelly Donut

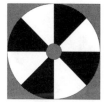

Bird's Eye View

Chariot Wheel

Wagon Wheel

Southern Star

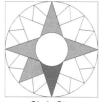

Circle Star

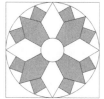

Courtyard

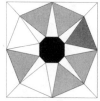

Rising Star

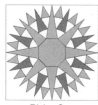

Rising Sun

Round Table

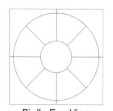

Bird's Eye View

Wheel of Fortune

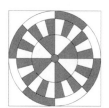

Wheel of Fortune

Diamond in the Square

Economy Patch

Twelve Triangles

Square in a Square

Mosaic

Double Cross

Triple Stripe

Mother's Dream

Susannah (Variation)

Susannah (Variation)

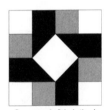

Susannah (Variation)

Weathervane

Improved Four Patch

Coffin Star

Grandmother's Cross

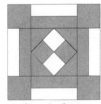

Coxey's Camp

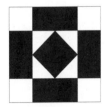

New Album

Art Square

Right and Left

Sugar Bowl

Cross with a Cross

King's Crown

Monkey Wrench

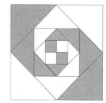

Snail's Trail

Contrary Wife

1 Classic Pieced
Dresden Fan

3 Petal
Dresden Flower Fan

4 Petal
Dresden Flower Fan

5 Petal
Dresden Flower Fan

6 Petal
Dresden Flower Fan

7 Petal
Dresden Flower Fan

8 Petal
Dresden Flower Fan

3 Petal Dresden Fan

4 Petal Dresden Fan

5 Petal Dresden Fan

6 Petal Dresden Fan

7 Petal Dresden Fan

8 Petal Dresden Fan

3 Petal Small Center
Dresden Fan

4 Petal Small Center
Dresden Fan

5 Petal Small Center
Dresden Fan

6 Petal Small Center
Dresden Fan

7 Petal Small Center
Dresden Fan

8 Petal Small Center
Dresden Fan

3 Petal Large Center
Dresden Fan

4 Petal Large Center
Dresden Fan

5 Petal Large Center
Dresden Fan

6 Petal Large Center
Dresden Fan

7 Petal Large Center
Dresden Fan

8 Petal Large Center
Dresden Fan

1 Classic Pieced
Dresden Plate

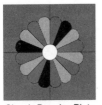

Classic Dresden Plate

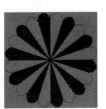

Dresden Flower

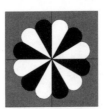

3 Petal Dresden Plate

4 Petal Dresden Plate

5 Petal Dresden Plate

6 Petal Dresden Plate

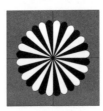

7 Petal Dresden Plate

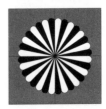

8 Petal Dresden Plate

3 Petal Small Center
Dresden Plate

4 Petal Small Center
Dresden Plate

5 Petal Small Center
Dresden Plate

6 Petal Small Center
Dresden Plate

7 Petal Small Center
Dresden Plate

8 Petal Small Center
Dresden Plate

3 Petal Large Center
Dresden Plate

4 Petal Large Center
Dresden Plate

5 Petal Large Center
Dresden Plate

6 Petal Large Center
Dresden Plate

7 Petal Large Center
Dresden Plate

8 Petal Large Center
Dresden Plate

1 Classic Pieced
Drunkard's Path

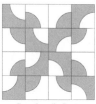

Drunkard's Path

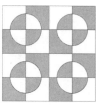

Indiana Puzzle

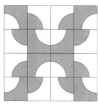

Falling Timbers

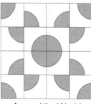

Around the World

Fool's Puzzle

Drunkard's Path

Drunkard's Path

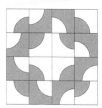

Dove

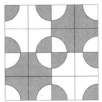

Millwheel

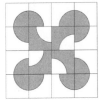

I Wish You Well

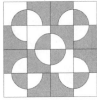

Drunkard's Path Var. I

Steeplechase

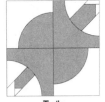

Turtle

Drunkard's Pinwheel

Peace Dove

Over the Bridge

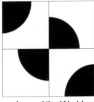

Around the World

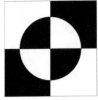

Baseball

1 Classic Pieced Eccentrics

Paducah Peony

Ribbons

Washington's Puzzle

Slashed Album

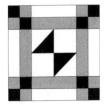

Odds and Ends

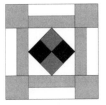

Coxey's Camp

Crossed Canoes

Ribbon Border

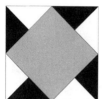
Right and Left

Work Box

Tangled Lines

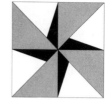
Double Pinwheel Whirls

Left and Right

Jewel

The Priscilla

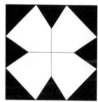
The Mayflower

1 Classic Pieced Eight-Point Stars

Star of the East

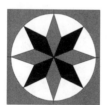
Royal Diamonds

Diamond

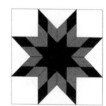
Blazing Star

Love in a Mist

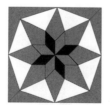
Pole Star

Octagon Star

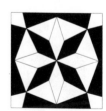
Octagon Star

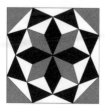
Western Spy

Octagon

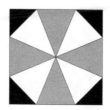
Kaleidoscope

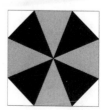
Kaleidoscope (2)

Silver and Gold

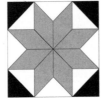

Eight-pointed Star

Lemoyne Star Var.

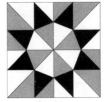

Star Var.

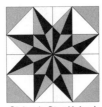

St. Louis Star (Adap.)

1 Classic Pieced
Five Patch

Cross and Crown

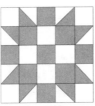

Four X Star

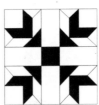

Goose Tracks

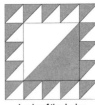

Lady of the Lake

Flying Squares

Square and a Half

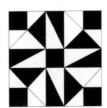

Pinwheel Square

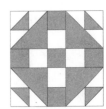

Duck and Ducklings

Handy Andy

Bird's Nest

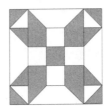

Fool's Square

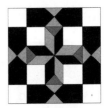

St. Louis Star

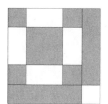

Children's Delight

King's Crown

Red Cross

Crazy House

Clown

Providence Quilt Block

Goose in the Pond

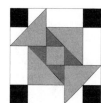

Grandmother's Puzzle

Sister's Choice

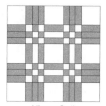

Album Quilt

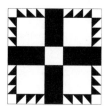

Premium Star

Fanny's Fan

Odd Scraps Patchwork

1 Classic Pieced
Four Patch

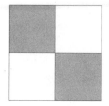

Four Patch

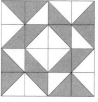

Whirlpool

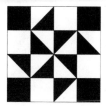

Flying-X

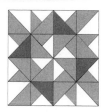

Windmill

Crown of Thorns

Temple Court

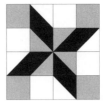
Clay's Choice

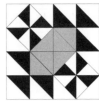
Hither & Yon

Fox & Geese

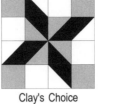
Hovering Hawks

Old Maid's Puzzle

Yankee Puzzle

Girl's Favorite

Girl's Favorite (2)

School Girl's Puzzle

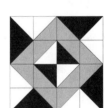
Blockade

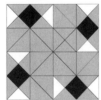
Flying Fist

Patch as Patch Can

Ladies' Aid Block

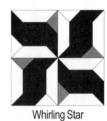
Whirling Star

Dogtooth Violet

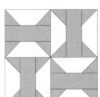
Arkansas Traveler

Kansas Troubles

Swing in the Center

Spools

Lattice Square

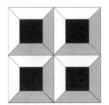
Red and White Cross

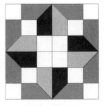
Lucky Clover

Four-Patch Var.

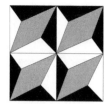

Blue Boutonnieres

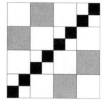

Carrie Nation Quilt

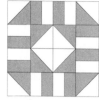

Cross Roads

Garret Windows

Vines at the Window

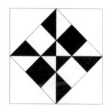

Storm Signal

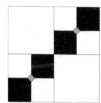

Dad's Bow Tie

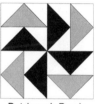

Dutchman's Puzzle

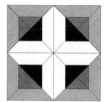

White Cross

Star and Cubes

School Girl's Puzzle

1 Classic Pieced
Ladies Art Company

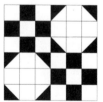

Flagstones

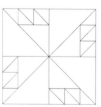

Rosebud

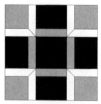

Hand Weave

All Kinds

Linton

Roman Cross

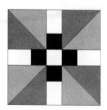

Propeller

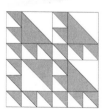

Lost Ship Pattern

Texas Flower

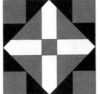
Cross Within Cross

Widower's Choice

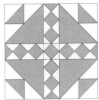
Bird's Nest

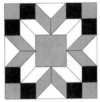
Merry Kite

Star of North Carolina

Navajo

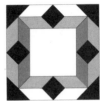
Baton Rouge Block

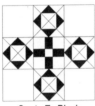
Santa Fe Block

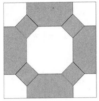
Magic Circle

Album

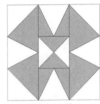
Double Z

Storm at Sea

Chicago Star

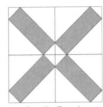
Devil's Puzzle

Star and Chains

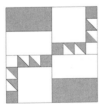
World's Fair Puzzle

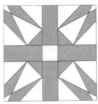
New Star

Wheel of Fortune

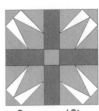
Crosses and Star

Bat's Wings

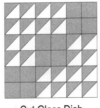
Cut Glass Dish

DoubleX, No. 1

DoubleX, No. 2

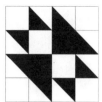

DoubleX, No. 3

DoubleX, No. 4

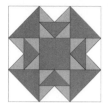

Capital T

Texas Tears

Old Maid's Ramble

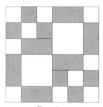

Domino

Letter H

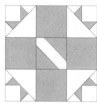

W.C.T. Union

Leap Frog

Steps to the Altar

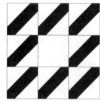

Nonsuch

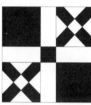

Widower's Choice

A Snowflake

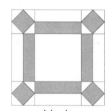

Johnnie-
Round-the-Corner

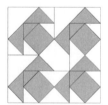

T Quartette

1 Classic Pieced
Nine Patch

Nine Patch

Hourglass I

Calico Puzzle

Attic Window

Contrary Wife

Friendship Star

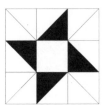

Eccentric Star

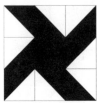

Eccentric Star 2

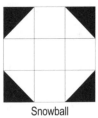

Eccentric Star

Eccentric Star 3

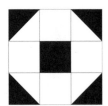

Snowball Variation

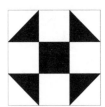

Shoo Fly

Snowball

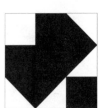

Darting Birds

Maple Leaf

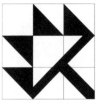

Cactus Bud

Practical Orchard

The Letter X

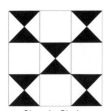

Clown's Choice

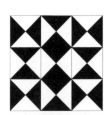

Aunt Malvernia's
Chain V.

Buckwheat

Arkansas Snowflake

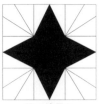

Time & Tide

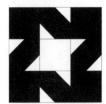

Mississippi

Nine-Patch Var.

Nine-Patch 2 Var.

Pinwheel Var.

Beggar Block

Optical Illusion

Letter X

Arkansas Snowflake

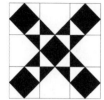

Cats and Mice

Rolling Stone

Broken Wheel

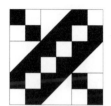

Road to California

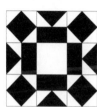

Rolling Squares

Kansas Star

Arbor Window

Storm Signal

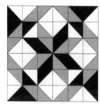

All Hallows

Wyoming Valley

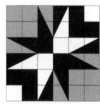

Bird of Paradise

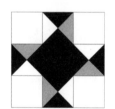

Stellie

Mollie's Choice

Joseph's Coat

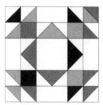

Summer Winds

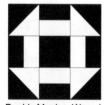

Double Monkey Wrench

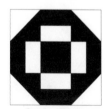

Grecian Square

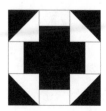

Greek Cross

Aunt Dinah

Shoo Fly

Saw Tooth

Five Spot

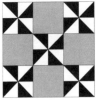

The Windmill

1 Classic Pieced
Nine Patch Stars

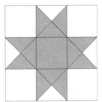

Variable Star

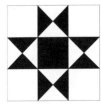

Aunt Eliza's Star

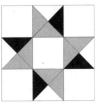

Twin Star

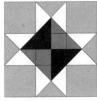

Country Farm

Star Variation

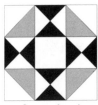

Swamp Angel

Card Basket

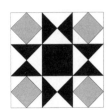

Ornate Star

Ribbon Quilt

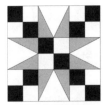

Garden Patch

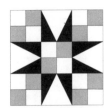

Fifty-Four-Forty...

Eight-pointed Star

Old Snowflake

Nine Patch Star

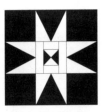

Dove at the Window

Nine Patch Star

Indiana Puzzle

 # 1 Classic Pieced
Old Favorites

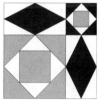

Storm at Sea

Chinese Lanterns

Pieced Bouquet

Nose-Gay

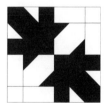

Silver Maple

Jewel Star

Starry Path

Road to Fortune

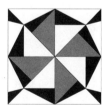

Lucky Star

Full Blown Tulip

Pineapple

The Palm

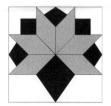

Cornucopia

Lotus Block

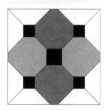

Meadow Flower

Friendship Bouquet

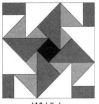

Whirligig

Double Windmill

Setting Sun

1 Classic Pieced
Orange Peels Etc.

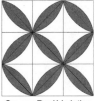

Orange Peel Variation

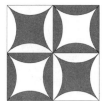

Sugar Bowl

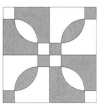

True Lover's Knot

Flowering Snowball

Papa's Delight

Raleigh

Clamshell

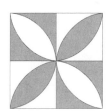

Flower Petals

Joseph's Coat

Snowball

Melon Patch

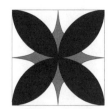

Alabama Beauty

Grist Mill

Four Leaf Clover

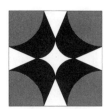

Friendship Circle

Spring Beauty

1 Classic Pieced
Picket Borders

Picket Border 1

Picket Border 2

Picket Border 3

Picket Border 4

Picket Border 5

Picket Border 6

Picket Border 7

Picket Border 8

Picket Border 9

Picket Border 10

Picket Border 11

Picket Border 12

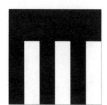

Picket Border 13

Picket Border 14

Picket Border 15

Picket Border 16

Sailboat Quilt

Boat

Airways

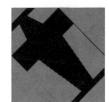

The Airplane

Jack's House

The Old Homestead

House on the Hill

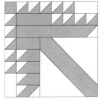

Proud Pine

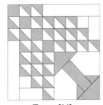

Tree of Life

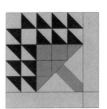

Pine Tree

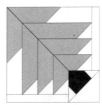

Pine Tree Quilt

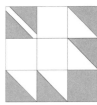

Maple Leaf

The Butterfly Quilt (2)

Butterfly

Grape Basket

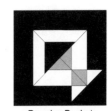

Dresden Basket

A Basket Quilt...

Cake Stand

Grandmother's Basket

Flower Pot

Butterfly

Pine Tree

Old Country Church

Forbidden Fruit Tree

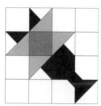

Vase of Flowers

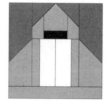

Red Barn

Bowl of Fruit

Log Cabin

Patch House

Little Red Schoolhouse

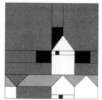

Dutch Mill

English Ivy

Dutch Boat

Trumpet Vine

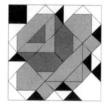

Rose

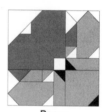

Pansy

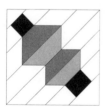

Lantern

Fruit Basket

1 Classic Pieced
Simple Blocks

Half-Square Triangle

Half-Square Triangle 2

Diagonal Strips

Diagonal Strips 2

Four Patch

Four-Patch Variation

Four-Patch Variation 2

Four-Patch Variation 3

Indian Hatchets

Indian Hatchets 2

Nine Patch

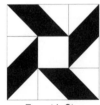

Eccentric Star

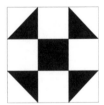

Shoo Fly

Eight-pointed Star

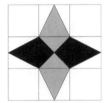

Arkansas Snowflake

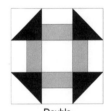

Double
Monkey Wrench

The Spool

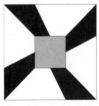

Formal Garden Variation

World Without End Var.

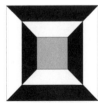

Box-in-a-Box Variation

The Diversion Quilt

Spool 2

Diamond in the Square

Economy Patch

Twelve Triangles

The Priscilla

Right and Left

Mosaic #3

New Album

Coffin Star

Improved Four Patch

Granny's Choice (Adap.)

Four X

Four X Var.

Windmill and Outline

Spinning Stars Var.

Twin Sisters

Whirlwind

The Mayflower

Bow Tie

Attic Window

Center Diamond Var.

Wild Goose Var.

Wild Goose 2 Var.

Wild Goose Chase

Wild Goose Chase

Wild Goose Chase

Wild Goose Chase

1 Classic Pieced Stars

Square and a Half

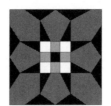

Klondike Star

Chicago Star

Providence Quilt Block

Uncle Sam's Hourglass

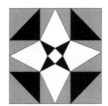

Little Rock Block

Star Variation

Split 12 Point Star

12 Point Star

Flower Star

Rolling Plate

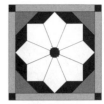

Fan Flower

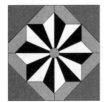

Purple Coneflower

Sunbeam

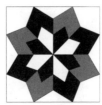

Double Star

Morning Star

1 Classic Pieced
Striped Borders

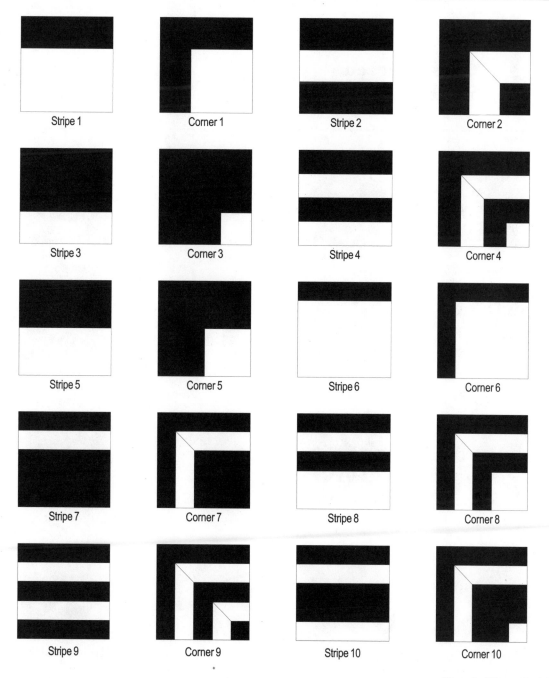

Stripe 1	Corner 1	Stripe 2	Corner 2
Stripe 3	Corner 3	Stripe 4	Corner 4
Stripe 5	Corner 5	Stripe 6	Corner 6
Stripe 7	Corner 7	Stripe 8	Corner 8
Stripe 9	Corner 9	Stripe 10	Corner 10

Stripe 11

Corner 11

Stripe 12

Corner 12

1 Classic Pieced
Traditional 4X

Basic 4X

Checkerboard

Boise

Cock's Comb

Aunt Melvernia's
Chain

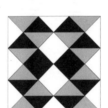

Buckwheat

Four X Var.

Granny's Choice
(Adap.)

The Arrowhead

Sarah's Favorite

New Hour Glass

Twin Sisters

Windmill and Outline

Criss Cross

Criss Cross Var.

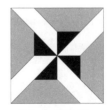

Spinning Stars Var.

Good Luck

 1 Classic Pieced Triangle Borders

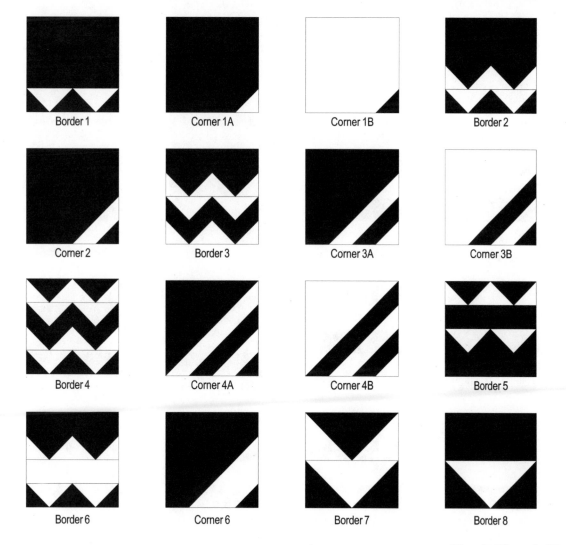

Border 1

Corner 1A

Corner 1B

Border 2

Corner 2

Border 3

Corner 3A

Corner 3B

Border 4

Corner 4A

Corner 4B

Border 5

Border 6

Corner 6

Border 7

Border 8

Corner 8A

Corner 8B

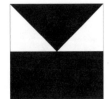

Border 9

Sawtooth Border 1

Double Sawtooth

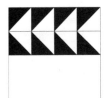

Wild Goose Chase
Border

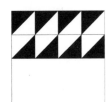

Diamond Border

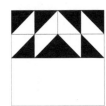

Diamond Border 2

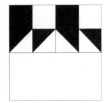

Check and Triangle
Border

Check and Triangle 2

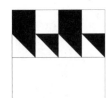

Check and Triangle 3

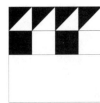

Check and Triangle 4

Stripe and Strips

Stripe and Strips II

Stripe and Strips III

Triangles and Strips

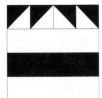

Triangles and Strips 2

Triangles and Strips 3

Diamonds and Strips

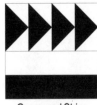

Geese and Strips

Meeting Geese
& Strips

Geese and Strips 2

Chevrons & Strips

Slanting Stripes
& Strips

Triple Slanting Strips

Zig Zags

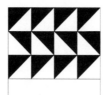

Triple Triangles

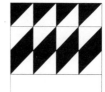

Double Diamonds

Meeting
Double Diamonds

Triangles

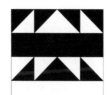

Meeting Triangles

Diamond in Square
Strips

Chevrons and Stripes

Meeting Chevrons

More
Diamonds & Strips

Double Diamonds 2

Diamonds & Triangles

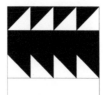

Up and Down
Triangles

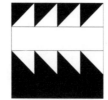

Tree Everlasting Border

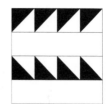

Tree Everlasting 2

Zig Zag 2

Zig Zag 3

Zig Zag 4

Zig Zag 5

2 Contemporary Pieced

2 Contemporary Pieced
Autograph Block Variations

January Autograph

February Autograph

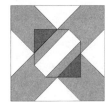

March Autograph

April Autograph

May Autograph

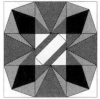

June Autograph

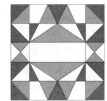

July Autograph

August Autograph

September Autograph

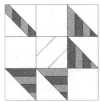

October Autograph

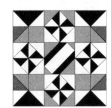

November Autograph

December Autograph

Monday Autograph

Tuesday Autograph

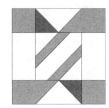

Wednesday Autograph

Thursday Autograph

2 Contemporary Pieced Baskets

Easter Basket

Topiary

Barbershop Baskets

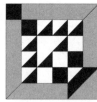

Checkerboard Basket

Basket Pinwheel

Postmodern Basket

Woven Basket

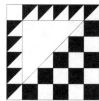

Berry Basket

Scrap Basket

Sun & Shadow Basket

Lily Basket

Amish Basket

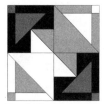

Sun & Shadow Baskets

Adirondack Baskets

Sugar Creek Basket

Rick-Rack Basket

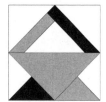

Brittany Basket

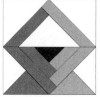

Log Cabin Basket

Charm Basket

Nine-patch Baskets

Megan's Baskets

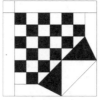
Berry Basket

Double-Baskets

Rick-Rack Basket

2 Contemporary Pieced
Cross Variations

Cross 1

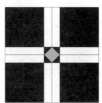
Cross 2

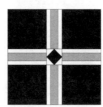
Cross 3

Cross 4

Cross 5

Cross 6

Cross 7

Cross 8

Cross 9

Cross 10

Cross 11

Cross 12

Cross 13

Cross 14

Cross 15

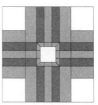
Cross 16

2 Contemporary Pieced Fans

Fanblades

Rainbow Fan

Floating Fan

Tie Fan

Diamond Diane's Fan

Leaf Fan

North Baltimore Fan

Louvre Fan

Jan's Fan

Petal Fan

Daisy Petal Fan

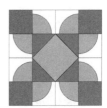

Fan Flower

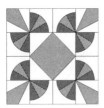

Butterfly Fan

Fan Dance

Fat Quarters Fan

Silk Rainbow

2 Contemporary Pieced Fauna

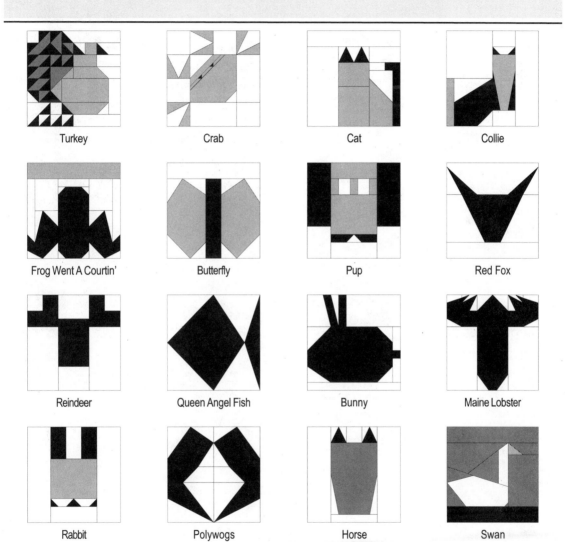

Turkey	Crab	Cat	Collie
Frog Went A Courtin'	Butterfly	Pup	Red Fox
Reindeer	Queen Angel Fish	Bunny	Maine Lobster
Rabbit	Polywogs	Horse	Swan

2 Contemporary Pieced Flags

Eight-Point Flag

Flag in a Box

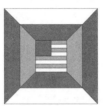

Flag in a Box II

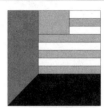

Attic Flag

Flag in the Square

Wild Goose Flag

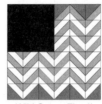

Wild Goose Flag II

Heart Flag

Heart Flag II

Log Cabin Flag

Log Cabin Flag II

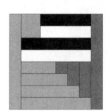

Log Cabin Flag III

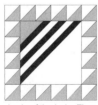

Lady of the Lake Flag

Whirlwind Flag

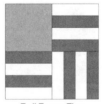

Rail Fence Flag

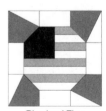

Pinwheel Flag

Buds and Ribbons

Blossom

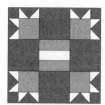

Sunflower

Peony

Amaryllis Bulb

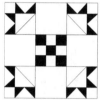

Picnic Bouquet

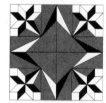

Daffodil Ring

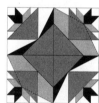

Alpine Flower

Floral Wreath

Rosebud

Rose

Foxglove

Foxglove Too

Tulip

Lily Block

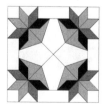

Lily Wreath

2 Contemporary Pieced
Good Alternative Blocks

9-patch Snowball

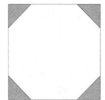

4-patch Snowball

Rail Fence Quilt

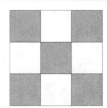

9-patch

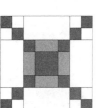

Chain 1

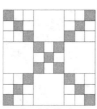

9-patch Chain

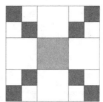

4-patch Chain

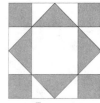

Economy

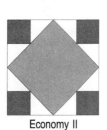

Economy II

Cross X

Uneven Cross X

Wide Cross X

Broken Sash Strip

Broken Sash Strip II

Broken Sash Strip III

Puss in the Corner

2 Contemporary Pieced Home Delights

Bathtub Boat

Hot Latte

Birthday Party

Happy Returns

Bird House

Good Morning

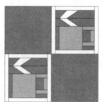

Good Night

He

She

Toy Barn

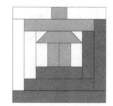

Log Cabin Doll

She and He by Judy Vigiletti

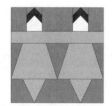

Two Friends by Judy Vigiletti

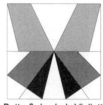

Butterfly by Judy Vigiletti

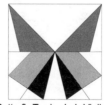

Butterfly Too by Judy Vigiletti

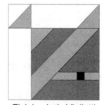

Fish by Judy Vigiletti

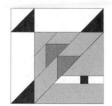

Fish Too by Judy Vigiletti

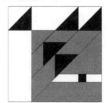

Fish Too II by Judy Vigiletti

Sewing Machine

Fabric Bolts

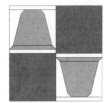

Thimbles

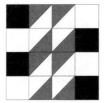

EQ Logo

Star of David (Debbie Sichel)

Star of David 2 (Debbie Sichel)

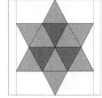

Star of David 3 (Debbie Sichel)

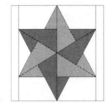

Star of David 4 (Debbie Sichel)

2 Contemporary Pieced Houses

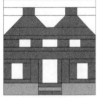

Brooklyn

St. Louis

Chicago

Baltimore

Milwaukee

Philadelphia

Detroit

Kansas City

Saltbox

Lighthouse

Prairie House

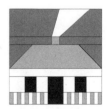

Picket Fence

Terrie's in Taos

Condo

Wisconsin Cabin

The Lake Cottage

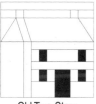

Old Two-Story

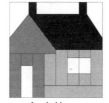

Ann's House

Country Cottage

2 Contemporary Pieced
Kaleidoscopes

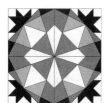

Rose Window

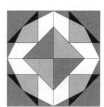

Diamond Bracelet

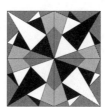

Dunce Caps

Alpine Flower

Electric Fan

Puzzle Ball

Pinball Swirl

Faceted Star

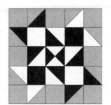

Modern Milky Way

Comet

Jupiter

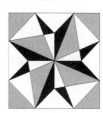

Cat's Tails

Rolling Crosses

Diamond Ring

Lobster Claws

Gemstone

2 Contemporary Pieced
Log Cabin-Like

Courthouse Stars

Rotary Ribbon

Strip Circles

Fan Rails

Round Cabin

Scrappy Stripper

Rainbow Logs

Starflower

Interlaced Logs

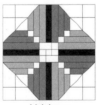

Irish Logs

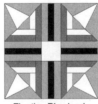

Floating Pinwheels

Lacy Lattice Work

Striped Lattice Work

High Flying Squares

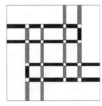

Plaid Lattice

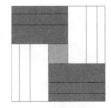

Woven Logs

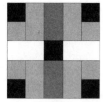

Plaid Fab

2 Contemporary Pieced
New Stars

String Star

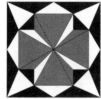

Hopatcong Star

Shadow Star

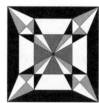

Sedona Star

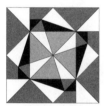

Mule Shoe TX

Bettina's Star

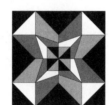

Cheyenne Star

Folded Star

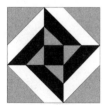

Strip Star

Propeller

Savannah Star

EQ's Stars & Beams

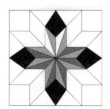

Star Var. 2

Star Var. 3

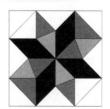

EQ Star

EQ Star 2

EQ Star 3

EQ Star 4

EQ Star 5

EQ Star 6

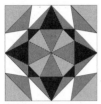

EQ Kaleidoscope Star

2 Contemporary Pieced
Pinwheels & Potpourri

Woven Lattice

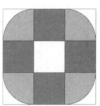

Button

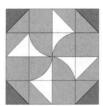

Electric Fan

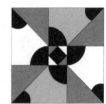

Scrap Blossoms

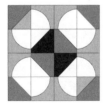

Fan Weaver

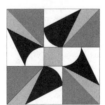

Windmill

Ucello's Shield

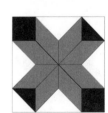

Costume Jewelry

Opening Gates

Belt Buckle

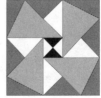

Origami

Walking X

Spinning Blades

Shining Bright

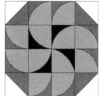

Jungle Flower

Cool Fan

2 Contemporary Pieced
Prairie Style

Wright

Stickley

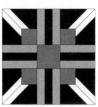

Eastlake

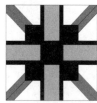

Lowey

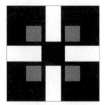

Downing

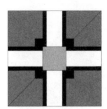

Bel Geddes

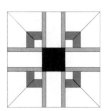

Teague

Dreyfuss

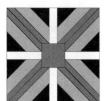

Sullivan

Burnham

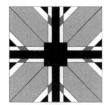

Fuller

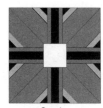

Gropius

Le Corbusier

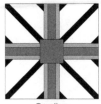

Bradley

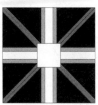

Roycroft

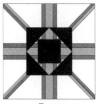

Fargo

2 Contemporary Pieced
Royal Crowns

Old Snowflake

Whirligig

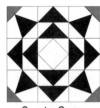
Country Crown

Meadow Flower

String Star

Crossing Winds

Tall Star

Jack of Diamonds

Scrap Violet

Galaxy

Rotate Me

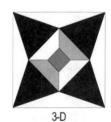
3-D

Illusion

Metalwork

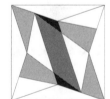
Metalwork Variation

Metalwork Variation II

Trading Post

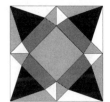

Harlequin

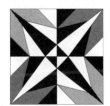

Jungle Star

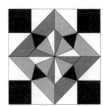

Windmill

Windmill II

Fireworks

Scrap Sparkler

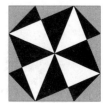

Tumbling Cube

Checked X

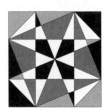

Emerging Star

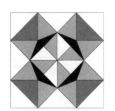

Faceted Star

Rolling Rock

Hourglass Puzzle

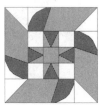

Star Swirl

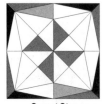

Secret Star

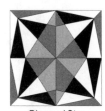

Diamond Star

Jupiter

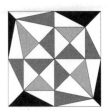

Uneven Star

Tumbling Star

2 Contemporary Pieced Spinning Suns

Black-Eyed Susan

Sun Spin

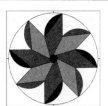

Star Dahlia

Kirsten's Star

Diamond Diane

September Flower

Nevada Star

Rhode Island Star

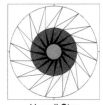

Hawaii Star

Dizzy Spinner

Blueberry Pie

Rhubarb Pie

Key Lime Pie

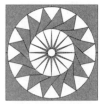

Raspberry Cream

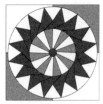

Cool Mint Candy

Fireworks

2 Contemporary Pieced Strip Quilts

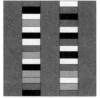

Strippy Bars

Roman Stripe

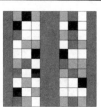

Striped Squares

Split Bars

Bits & Pieces

Random Stripes

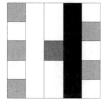

Random Stripes II

Mexican Blanket

Picket and Posts

Fancy Fence

Candy Canes

Waving Flag

Lightening Strips

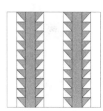

Tree Everlasting

Scrap Chevrons

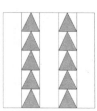

Wild Goose Chase

2 Contemporary Pieced Sun Compasses

Sun Compass 1

Sun Compass 2

Sun Compass 3

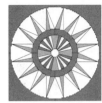

Sun Wheel 1

Sun Circle

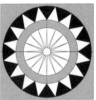

Prairie Point Sun

Sun Wheel 2

Star within Sun

South Pole Star

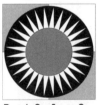

Dean's Sunflower Sun

August Sun

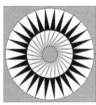

Sun Swirl

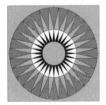

Sun Spokes

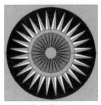

Sun Rings

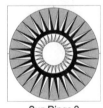

Sun Rings 2

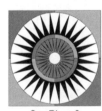

Sun Rings 3

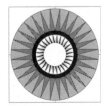

Sun Rings 4

Sedona's Sun

Blue Shirt

Shirt & Sweater

Starched Shirt

Work Shirt

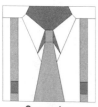

Suspenders

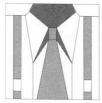

Executive

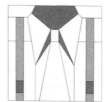

The Harvard Club

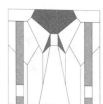

Country Lawyer

T-Shirt

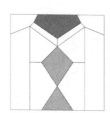

Logo T-Shirt

No Tie Shirt

Shirt and Sweater

Stuffed Shirt

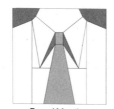

Bored Meeting

Pocket Protector

Cowboy Shirt

2 Contemporary Pieced Trees

Sweet Gum

Snowy Pine

Sugar Maple

Hemlock

Pinwheel Pine

Christmas Pine

Mulberry Bush

Blue Spruce

Birds in the Pine

Log Cabin Tree

Old Oak

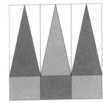

Topiary Trio

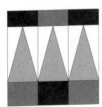

Topiary Trio Too

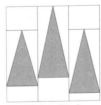

Topiary Trio 3

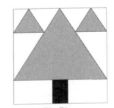

Big Pine

Evergreen

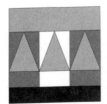

Three Trees

Big & Little Trees

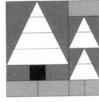

Striped Big & Little

Triangle Tree

Triangle Tree II

Tree in the Forest

Crab Apple

Red Maple

Diamond-in-the-Tree

Geometric Tree

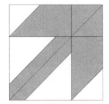

Willow

Blue Spruce

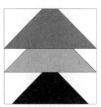

Blue Spruce II

Umbrella Tree

Tree on a Hill

3 Paper Piecing

Basket

Striped Basket

On-point Basket

On-point Basket II

On-point Basket III

On-point Basket IV

Basket on the Table

Bowl on Striped Cloth

Striped Bowl on Cloth

Basket

Big Basket

Big Striped Basket

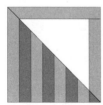

On-point Layered Basket

On-point Layered Basket II

Curved-handle Basket

Layered Basket

3 Paper Piecing
Crazy Foundations

Crazy I

Crazy II

Crazy III

Crazy IV

Crazy V

Crazy VI

Crazy VII

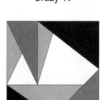

Crazy VIII

Crazy IX

Crazy X

Crazy XI

Crazy XII

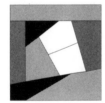

Crazy XIII

Crazy XIV

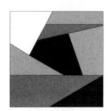

Crazy XV

Crazy XVI

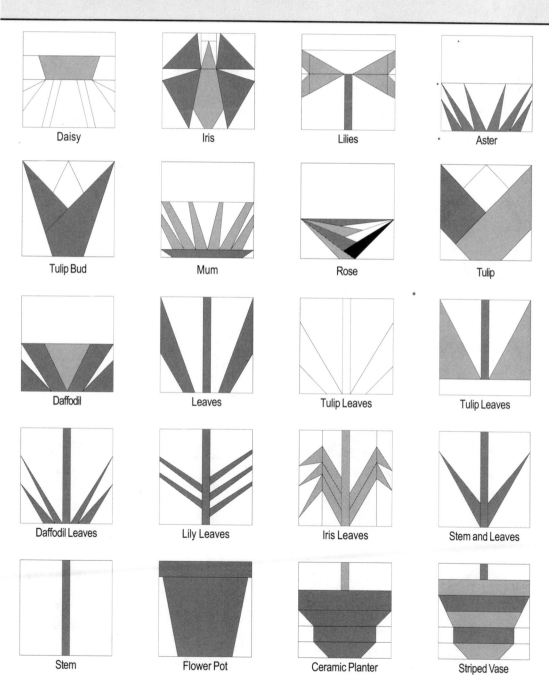

Daisy

Iris

Lilies

Aster

Tulip Bud

Mum

Rose

Tulip

Daffodil

Leaves

Tulip Leaves

Tulip Leaves

Daffodil Leaves

Lily Leaves

Iris Leaves

Stem and Leaves

Stem

Flower Pot

Ceramic Planter

Striped Vase

Crocus

Snowdrop

Bluebell

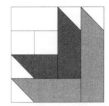

Double Tulip

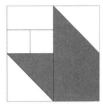

Yellow Tulip

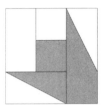

Red Tulip

Daffodil

Leafstem 1

Leafstem 2

3 Paper Piecing
Flying Geese

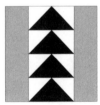

Flying Geese

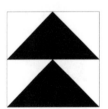

Flying Geese I

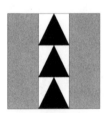

Flying Geese II

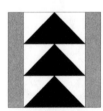

Flying Geese III

Flying Geese IV

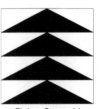

Flying Geese V

Flying Geese VI

Flying Geese VII

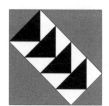

Flying Geese VIII

Flying Geese IX

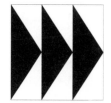

Flying Geese X

Flying Geese XI

Flying Geese XII

Flying Geese XIII

Flying Goose

Flying Goose Var.

3 Paper Piecing
Fun Stuff

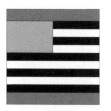

Flag

Schooner

Snake

Sunrise

On-point Flag

On-point Flag II

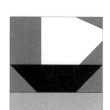

Sailboat

Sailboat II

Sailboat III

Big Bird House

Cat Head

Rabbit Head

Dog Head

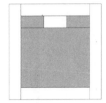
Bear Head

Mouse (EQ) Head

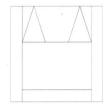
Fox Head

Elf Cottage

Elf Asleep

Elf Tree

Another Elf Tree

Tiny House

House Beneath the Bridge

Topsy-Turvy House

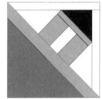
Tiny House Too

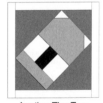
Another Tiny Tree

Elf Boat

3 Paper Piecing
Geometrics

Rail Fence

Rail Fence II

Rail Fence III

Diagonal Strips

Diagonal Strips II

Blocks in a Box

Blocks in a Box Var.

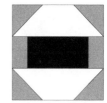

American Chain

Quarter Log Cabin

Cracker

Letter H

Diamond in the Square

Economy Patch

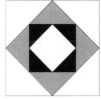

Twelve Triangles

Album

Album II

Broken Band Variation

3 Paper Piecing
Hebrew Alphabet (Debbie Sichel)

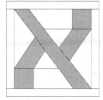

Aleph (Debbie Sichel)

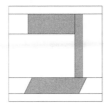

Bet (Debbie Sichel)

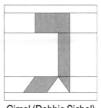

Gimel (Debbie Sichel)

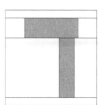

Dalet (Debbie Sichel)

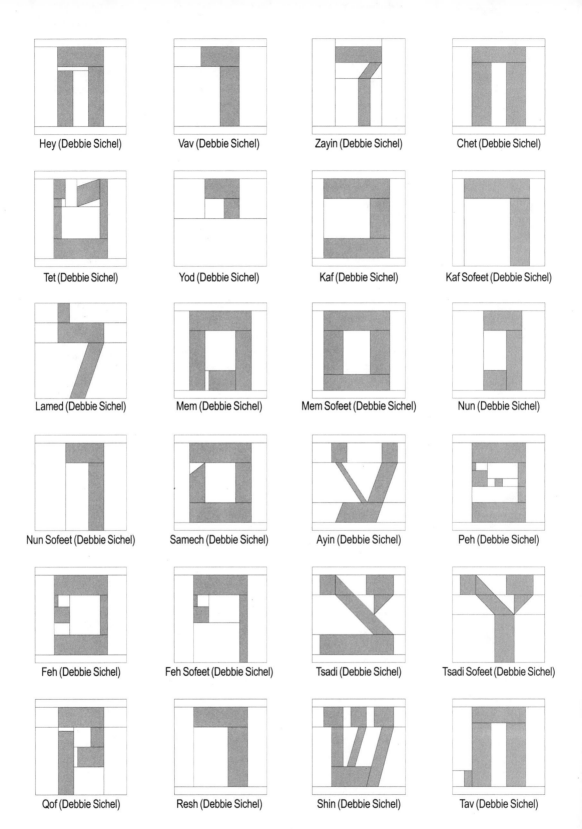

Hey (Debbie Sichel)

Vav (Debbie Sichel)

Zayin (Debbie Sichel)

Chet (Debbie Sichel)

Tet (Debbie Sichel)

Yod (Debbie Sichel)

Kaf (Debbie Sichel)

Kaf Sofeet (Debbie Sichel)

Lamed (Debbie Sichel)

Mem (Debbie Sichel)

Mem Sofeet (Debbie Sichel)

Nun (Debbie Sichel)

Nun Sofeet (Debbie Sichel)

Samech (Debbie Sichel)

Ayin (Debbie Sichel)

Peh (Debbie Sichel)

Feh (Debbie Sichel)

Feh Sofeet (Debbie Sichel)

Tsadi (Debbie Sichel)

Tsadi Sofeet (Debbie Sichel)

Qof (Debbie Sichel)

Resh (Debbie Sichel)

Shin (Debbie Sichel)

Tav (Debbie Sichel)

3 Paper Piecing
Holiday Foundations

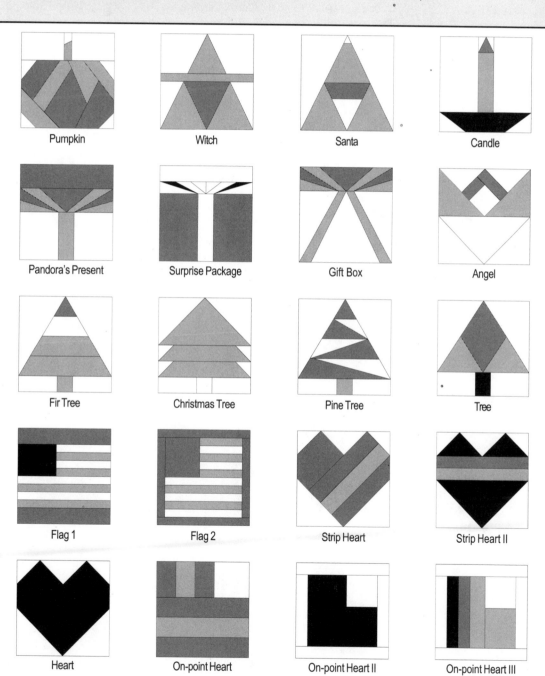

Pumpkin	Witch	Santa	Candle
Pandora's Present	Surprise Package	Gift Box	Angel
Fir Tree	Christmas Tree	Pine Tree	Tree
Flag 1	Flag 2	Strip Heart	Strip Heart II
Heart	On-point Heart	On-point Heart II	On-point Heart III

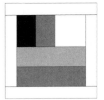

On-point Heart IV

On-point Heart V

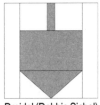

Dreidel (Debbie Sichel)

Grogger (Debbie Sichel)

Grogger 2 (Debbie Sichel)

3 Paper Piecing
In the Woods

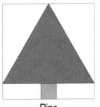

Pine

Fir

Little House

Log Cabin

Cabin

Under the Rainbow

Easy Leaf

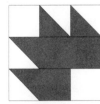

Maple Leaf

Maple Leaf

Leaf

Silver Maple

Oak Leaf

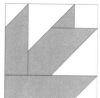
Red Oak

Sweetgum

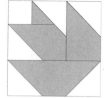
Maple

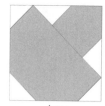
Ivy

Lily Pad

3 Paper Piecing
Log Cabins

Off-Center Log Cabin

Wild Goose Log Cabin

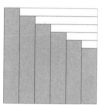
Quarter Cabin

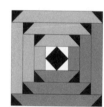
Diamond-in-Sq. L.Cabin

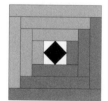
Diamond Center L.C.

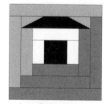
Log Cabin House

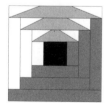
Log Cabin Pine

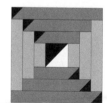
Marching Triangles

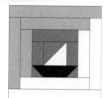
Log Cabin Boat

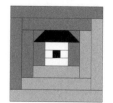
Wren House

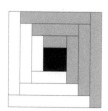
Log Cabin

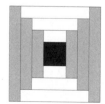
Courthouse Steps

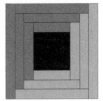

Large Center Log Cabin

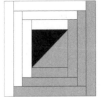

Split Center Log Cabin

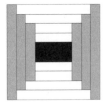

Rect. Center Log Cabin

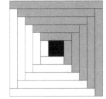

Log Cabin

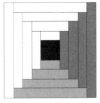

Log Cabin

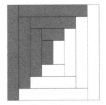

Log Cabin

Crazy Log Cabin

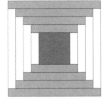

Courthouse Steps II

3 Paper Piecing
Pineapples

Pineapple

Pineapple II

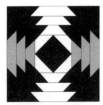

Pineapple III

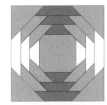

Pineapple IV

Pineapple V

Pineapple VI

Pineapple VII

Pineapple VIII

Pineapple IX

Pineapple X

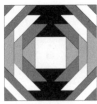

Pineapple XI

Pineapple Album

Pineapple Album II

Pineapple Album III

Pineapple Album IV

Pineapple Album V

3 Paper Piecing Trees

Tall Pines

Tall Tree

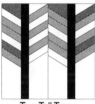
Two Tall Trees

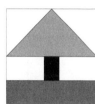
Evergreen

Evergreen I

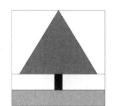
Evergreen II

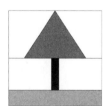
Evergreen III

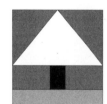
Evergreen IV

Evergreen & Shadow

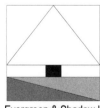
Evergreen & Shadow II

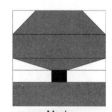
Maple

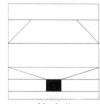
Maple II

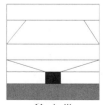
Maple III

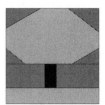
Maple IV

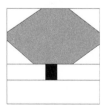
Maple V

Umbrella Tree

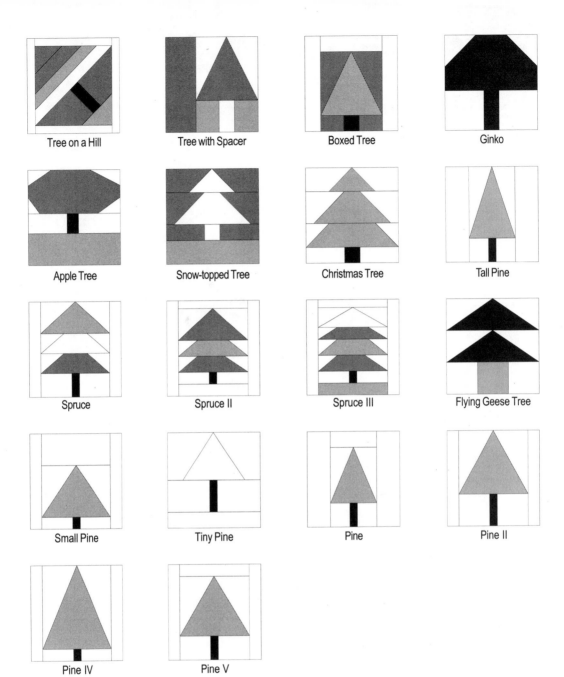

Tree on a Hill

Tree with Spacer

Boxed Tree

Ginko

Apple Tree

Snow-topped Tree

Christmas Tree

Tall Pine

Spruce

Spruce II

Spruce III

Flying Geese Tree

Small Pine

Tiny Pine

Pine

Pine II

Pine IV

Pine V

3 Paper Piecing
Twists

Twist I

Twist II

Twist III

Twist IV

Twist V

Twist VI

Twist VII

Twist VIII

Twist IX

Twist X

Twist XI

Twist XII

Twist XIII

Twist XIV

Twist XV

Twist XVI

Twist XVII

Twist XVIII

Twist XIX

Twist XX

Twist XXI

Twist XXII

Twist XXIII

Twist XXIV

Economy Patch

4 Classic Applique

4 Classic Applique
Crossing Designs

Lily Ring

Crossing Branches

Trellis Vines

Bottle Brush

Bud Block

Peonies

English Rose

English Rose II

19th-century Leaves

Baltimore Block

Lollipop Flowers

Oak Leaf & Reel

Oak Leaf Wreath

Oak Leaf Wreath II

Oak Leaf Wreath III

Mexican Rose

Mexican Rose

Circle Rose

Circle Rose II

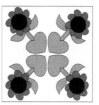

Hearts & Sunflowers

Crossing Roses

Comb

 4 Classic Applique
Grape & Vine Borders

Grapevine

Grapevine II

Grapevine III

Grapevine IV

Border Stem

Border Stem II

Border Stem III

Border Stem IV

Border Stem V

Border Stem VI

Border Stem VII

Border Stem VIII

Border Stem IX

Straight Stem

Corner Stem

Corner Stem II

4 Classic Applique
On-Point Flowers

First-place Flower

Rose & Buds

Three-Part Flower

Three-Part Flower II

Stencil Tulips

Tulip Tree

Large Tulip

Posey

Pennsylvania Dutch

Folk Tulip

Mexican Rose

Rose

4 Classic Applique
Sunbonnet Sue & Pals

Sunbonnet Sue

Valentine Sue

Bashful Sam

Sue Picks Tulips

Sunny Jim

Overall Bill

Sue Redux

Sue On-Point

Sue with Balloons

Sam

Bird

Cow

4 Classic Applique Wreaths

Valentine Wreath

Hearts & Ribbons

Forget-Me-Not Ring

Ribbon Medallion

Nosegay Wreath

Forget-Me-Not Wreath

Rose Wreath

Rose Wreath II

Rose of Sharon Wreath

Cabbage Rose Wreath

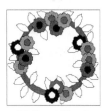

Wildflower Wreath

Wildflower Ring

Rose Ring

Tulip Ring

Flower Wreath

Flower Wreath II

Reel

5 Contemporary Applique

5 Contemporary Applique
Animals

Sheep

Butterfly

Butterflies

Butterflies and Blossom

Butterfly II

Butterfly III

Bluebird on Branch

Robin on Branch

Birdhouse

Birdhouse II

Horse

Pig

Elephant

Goose

Duck

Duckling

Duck II

Cardinal

Bird

Bird II

Giraffe

Starfish

Angel Fish

5 Contemporary Applique
Celtic Blocks

Celtic Patch

Celtic Patch 2

Celtic Patch 3

Celtic Patch 4

Celtic Patch 5

Puzzle Patch

Celtic Patch 6

Celtic Patch 7

Interlocking Squares

Ring Chain (corner)

Interlocking Squares (border)

Interlocking Rings (border)

Interlocking Rings

5 Contemporarary Applique
Christmas

Nutcracker

Angel with Candle

Rudolph the Red-Nosed Reindeer

Poinsettia

Ann's Angel

Candle and Holder

Christmas Tree

Tree in the Snow

Snowman Painting

Frosty

Snowman

Holly

Candle

Wreath

Mittens

Candy Cane

Bow

Christmas Tree

Hen

Nest with Eggs

Heart

Dress on a Clothesline

Dotted Dress

Dress with Buttons

Beet

Carrot

Turnip

Eggplant

Tomato

Radish

Seed Packet Row Marker

Seed Packet Row Marker II

Butterfly

Wiggly Star

Straight Star

Curly Flower

Curly Flower with Center

Flower

5 Contemporary Applique
Flowers

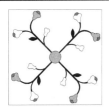

Blue Buds

Summer Block

Anemones

Roses and Butterfly

Posey and Butterfly

Two Buds

Two Buds 2

Blue Buds (quarter design)

Summer Block (quarter design)

Bird in the Buds

Dahlia

Rose

Poppies

Anemones (quarter design)

Shamrocks

Bouquet

5 Contemporary Applique
Flowers 2

Flower in the Grass

Daisy

Peony

Three-Part Flower

Three-Part Flower II

Rose and Buds

Rosebud

Stencil Tulips

Tulip Block

Tulip Block II

Flower Pot

Flower Pot II

Tyrolean Design

Wildflower Bouquet

Large Tulip

Tulip Tree

5 Contemporary Applique
Garden Blocks

Watering Can

Sunflowers in a Pot

Strawberry

Pea Pods on Vine

Bird on a Fence

Ann's Garden Wreath

Apple

Painted Pot

Tree of Life

Sunflower Fence

Watermelon Slice

Split Heart

Birdhouse

Butterfly

Ladybug

Flying Home

Peas in Pods

Pea Pod

5 Contemporary Applique
Hearts

Hearts and Doves

Stars and Hearts Forever

Heart with Candybox Ruffle

Heart of Leaves

Heart Ring

Garden of Hearts

Celtic Hearts with Leaves

Celtic Hearts

Heart Flower Bouquet

Single Celtic Heart

Gumdrop Heart

Four Hearts

Four Hearts

Double Hearts

Four Hearts II

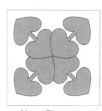

Heart Blossoms

Broken Heart

Heart Flower II

Heart Flower

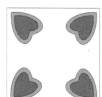

Corner Hearts

Eight Hearts

Crossing Hearts

5 Contemporary Applique
Music

"88" (Rita Denenberg)

Sax (Rita Denenberg)

Drum (Rita Denenberg)

Musical Signs (Rita Denenberg)

Violin (Rita Denenberg)

Big Bass (Rita Denenberg)

Clarinet (Rita Denenberg)

The Maestro (Rita Denenberg)

Treble Clef

Treble Staff

Bass Clef

Bass Staff

Guitar

Saxophone

Saxophone with Notes

Violin

Trumpet

Piano

Drum and Sticks

Musical Note I

Musical Note II

Musical Note III

5 Contemporary Applique
R Denenberg Christmas/Hanukkah

Peace Dove
(Rita Denenberg)

Angel
(Rita Denenberg)

Christmas Tree
(Rita Denenberg)

Wise Men
(Rita Denenberg)

Presents
(Rita Denenberg)

Christ Child
(Rita Denenberg)

Christmas Stocking
(Rita Denenberg)

Fireplace at Christmas
(Rita Denenberg)

Poinsettia Border
(Rita Denenberg)

Cardinal Corner
(Rita Denenberg)

Ring Those Bells
(Rita Denenberg)

Noel
(Rita Denenberg)

Wreath
(Rita Denenberg)

Coming Home
(Rita Denenberg)

Hanukkah
(Rita Denenberg)

David Star
(Rita Denenberg)

Dreidel
(Rita Denenberg)

5 Contemporary Applique
R Denenberg Easter & Halloween

Easter Basket
(Rita Denenberg)

Easter Egg
(Rita Denenberg)

Easter Rabbit 1
(Rita Denenberg)

Easter Rabbit 2
(Rita Denenberg)

Easter Rabbit 3
(Rita Denenberg)

Chick
(Rita Denenberg)

Easter Egg 2
(Rita Denenberg)

Easter Lily
(Rita Denenberg)

Bunny with Tulip
(Rita Denenberg)

Teddy Bear with Tulip
(Rita Denenberg)

Bunny with Egg
(Rita Denenberg)

Witch
(Rita Denenberg)

Black Cat
(Rita Denenberg)

Trick R Treat
(Rita Denenberg)

Jack O'Lantern
(Rita Denenberg)

Ghost
(Rita Denenberg)

Bats in Web
(Rita Denenberg)

5 Contemporary Applique
Rita Denenberg Garden

Carnation
(Rita Denenberg)

Lily
(Rita Denenberg)

Pansy
(Rita Denenberg)

Tiger Lily
(Rita Denenberg)

Garden Gate
(Rita Denenberg)

Lily of the Valley
(Rita Denenberg)

Gardenia
(Rita Denenberg)

Sunflower
(Rita Denenberg)

Rose
(Rita Denenberg)

Peony
(Rita Denenberg)

Lilacs
(Rita Denenberg)

Daffodil
(Rita Denenberg)

Bleeding Heart
(Rita Denenberg)

Iris - vertical
(Rita Denenberg)

Iris - on point
(Rita Denenberg)

Our Vase
(Rita Denenberg)

5 Contemporary Applique
Rita Denenberg Heart & Home

Lady Sue
(Rita Denenberg)

Biker
(Rita Denenberg)

Sunbonnet
(Rita Denenberg)

Geisha
(Rita Denenberg)

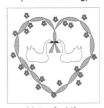

Mates for Life
(Rita Denenberg)

Family Tree
(Rita Denenberg)

Our House
(Rita Denenberg)

Peonies and Lilacs
(Rita Denenberg)

Heart of My Hearts
(Rita Denenberg)

We Grew Roses
(Rita Denenberg)

Our Wedding
(Rita Denenberg)

Dove Corner Block
(Rita Denenberg)

Rose Border
(Rita Denenberg)

Wreath
(Rita Denenberg)

Antique Birdcage
(Rita Denenberg)

Information Please
(Rita Denenberg)

My Hearts of Hearts
(Rita Denenberg)

 # 5 Contemporary Applique
Sports

Football

Basketball

Baseball

Soccer ball

Football
(Rita Denenberg)

Baseball
(Rita Denenberg)

Ice Skates
(Rita Denenberg)

Golfball
(Rita Denenberg)

Football Helmet
(Rita Denenberg)

Bowling Ball
(Rita Denenberg)

Bowling Pin
(Rita Denenberg)

The 18th Hole
(Rita Denenberg)

Gone Fishin'
(Rita Denenberg)

Roller Blade
(Rita Denenberg)

Baseball Cap
(Rita Denenberg)

Boxing Gloves
(Rita Denenberg)

Basketball Hoop
(Rita Denenberg)

You're #1
(Rita Denenberg)

Football Helmet

 **5 Contemporary Applique
Starry Night**

Lone Star

Man in the Moon

Little Dipper

Cloud

Big Dipper

Two Clouds

Thundercloud

Sun

Twinkling Stars

Twinkling Stars II

Starburst

Three Clouds

Star Group

Moon n Stars

Stars Above

Constellation

Crescent Moon

Star Group II

Sun 2

Wreathmaker Sun #1

5 Contemporary Applique
Toys

Train Engine Wind-up

Jack-in-the-Box

Clown Doll

Duck Pull-toy

Rocket

Robot I

Robot II

Spaceman Doll

World Globe

Toy Rocket

Carousel Horse
(Rita Denenberg)

Plane
(Rita Denenberg)

Bike

Tractor

Sailboat

Sailboat II

Sailboat III

Car

Plane

Rocket

Hammer

Wrench

Ted

Ted E. Bear

Circle Bear

5 Contemporary Applique
Your Design Studio

Me
(Rita Denenberg)

Needle & Thread
(Rita Denenberg)

Spool of Thread
(Rita Denenberg)

Patches
(Rita Denenberg)

Scissors
(Rita Denenberg)

Pincushion
(Rita Denenberg)

Rotary Cutter
(Rita Denenberg)

Thimble
(Rita Denenberg)

Sewing Machine

Bolt of Fabric

Spool of Thread

Computer Monitor

Keyboard

Telephone

Mouse and Pad

Magnifying Glass

CD

Floppy

Non-pc Computer

Computer Tower

6 Applique Motifs

Butterfly

Butterfly II

Butterfly III

Butterfly IV

Butterflies

Butterflies and Blossom

Bluebird on Branch

Robin on Branch

Cardinal

Bird

Bird II

Bird in the Buds

Ladybug

Birdhouse

Sheep

Horse

Pig

Elephant

Giraffe

Angel Fish

Duck

Goose

Duckling

Duck II

Starfish

 # 6 Applique Motifs (Layer 2)
Flower Heads

Sunflower

Double Tulip

Tulip and Leaves

Tulip Heads

Rose of Sharon

Zinnia

Pansy

Daffodil

Bud and Berries

Daisy

Blossoms

Violet Nosegay

Carnation

Jonquil

Orchid

Peony

6 Applique Motifs (Layer 2)
Flowers on Stems

Gloxinia

Posey

Small Tulip

Pennsylvania Dutch

Folk Tulip

Rose

Circle Rose

Mexican Rose

Coneflower

Coneflower II

Black-Eyed Susan

English Rose

Sunflower in Heart

Fantasy Flower

Daisy

Tulip

Strawberry

Cherries

Apple

Pear

Grapes

Orange

Beet

Carrot

Turnip

Eggplant

Tomato

Radish

Watermelon Slice

Pea Pod

Peas in Pods

Corn on the Cob

6 Applique Motifs (Layer 2)
Leaves & Stems

Maple Leaf

Dozen-leaf Stem

Dozen-leaf Stem II

Dozen-leaf Stem III

Eleven-leaf Stem

Sycamore Leaf

Leaf Sprig

Laurel Leaves

13-leaf Stem

Long Leaf

Oak Leaf

Stem & Leaves

Stem & Leaves

Petals

Flower

Stem

Stem with Branches

Stem & Branches

Stem

Sun

Heart

Star

Moon

Flower

Leaf

Ice Cream Cone

Tent

Balloons

Moorish Design

Happy Face

House

Tree

Apple Tree

Rainbow

Ball

6 Applique Motifs (Layer 2)
Sports

Basketball

Football

Baseball

Golfball
(Rita Denenberg)

Bowling Ball
(Rita Denenberg)

Bowling Pin
(Rita Denenberg)

You're #1
(Rita Denenberg)

Football Helmet

Ice Skate
(Rita Denenberg)

The 18th Hole
(Rita Denenberg)

Gone Fishin'
(Rita Denenberg)

Roller Blade
(Rita Denenberg)

Boxing Gloves
(Rita Denenberg)

Basketball Hoop
(Rita Denenberg)

Baseball Cap
(Rita Denenberg)

Baseball and Bat

6 Applique Motifs (Layer 2)
Starry Night

Snow-covered Tree

Man in the Moon

Little Dipper

Cloud

Big Dipper

Two Clouds

Twinkling Stars

Three Clouds

Star Group

Moon

Snow-covered Cabin

Smoke

Star

Moon N Stars

Moonlight

Moonlight II

6 Applique Motifs (Layer 2)
Sunbonnet Sue Motifs

Sunbonnet Sue

Valentine Sue

Bashful Sam

Sue Picks Tulips

Sunny Jim

Overall Bill

Sue Redux

Sue with Balloons

Sam

Bird

Cow

7 Quilting Stencils

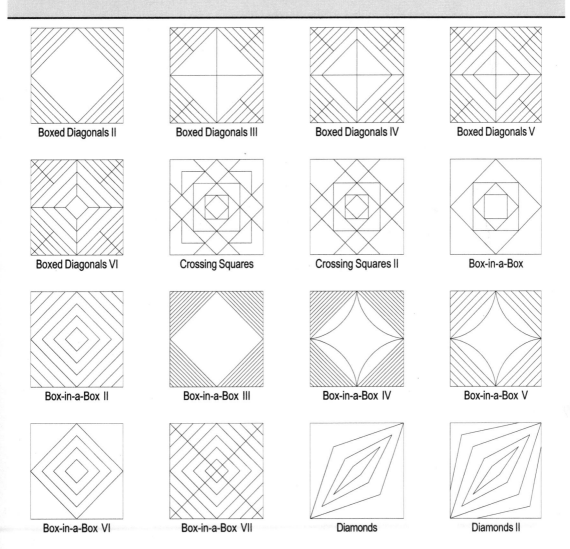

Boxed Diagonals II	Boxed Diagonals III	Boxed Diagonals IV	Boxed Diagonals V
Boxed Diagonals VI	Crossing Squares	Crossing Squares II	Box-in-a-Box
Box-in-a-Box II	Box-in-a-Box III	Box-in-a-Box IV	Box-in-a-Box V
Box-in-a-Box VI	Box-in-a-Box VII	Diamonds	Diamonds II

Celtic Circle

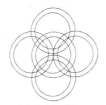

Interlocking Rings

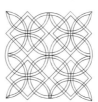

Rings and Squares

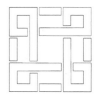

Celtic Interweave

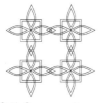

Celtic Squares and Loops

Celtic Rope

Rings and Squares 2

Celtic Squares and Loops 2

Interwoven Square

Looped Rings

Interlocking Squares

Celtic Squares and Loops 3

Ring Chain (corner)

Interlocking Rings (border)

Interlocking Rings

Interlocking Squares (border)

7 Quilting Stencils (Layer 3) Curves

Wineglass

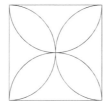

Wineglass II

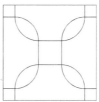

Interlocking Lines

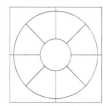

Wheel

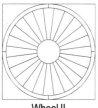

Wheel II

Circle-in-a Circle

Circle-in-a Circle II

Off-side Circles

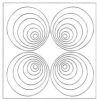

Four Off-Side Circles

Pumpkin Seeds

Pumpkin Seeds II

Pumpkin Seeds III

Clover

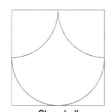

Clamshell

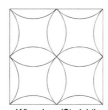

Wineglass (Straight)

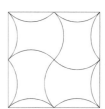

Seeds and Waves

7 Quilting Stencils (Layer 3)
Feathers

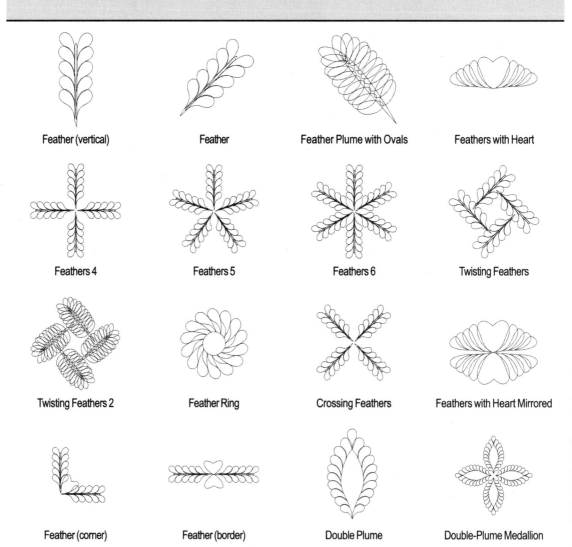

Feather (vertical)	Feather	Feather Plume with Ovals	Feathers with Heart
Feathers 4	Feathers 5	Feathers 6	Twisting Feathers
Twisting Feathers 2	Feather Ring	Crossing Feathers	Feathers with Heart Mirrored
Feather (corner)	Feather (border)	Double Plume	Double-Plume Medallion

7 Quilting Stencils (Layer 3)
Hearts

Staggered Hearts

Dozen Hearts

Nine Hearts

Double-Heart Ring

Heart Ring

Heart Ring 2

Heart Stars

Six Star Ring

Six Heart Ring 2

Heart Tulip Ring

Rolling Hearts

Rolling Hearts 2

Rolling Hearts 3

Rolling Hearts 4

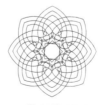

Rose Window

Double-Crossed Hearts

7 Quilting Stencils (Layer 3)
Hearts, Ribbons, Leaves

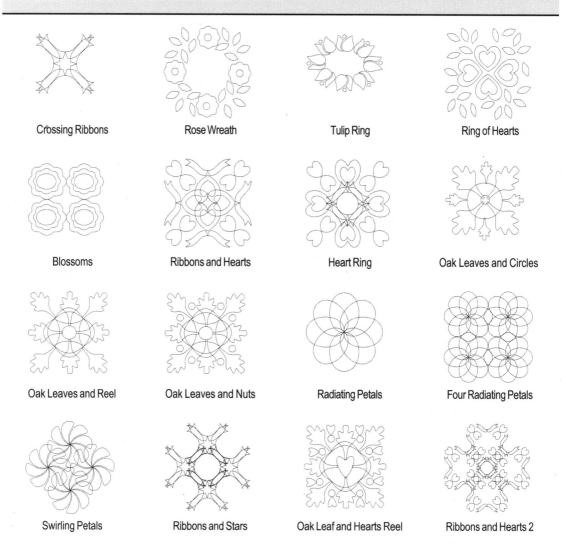

Crossing Ribbons	Rose Wreath	Tulip Ring	Ring of Hearts
Blossoms	Ribbons and Hearts	Heart Ring	Oak Leaves and Circles
Oak Leaves and Reel	Oak Leaves and Nuts	Radiating Petals	Four Radiating Petals
Swirling Petals	Ribbons and Stars	Oak Leaf and Hearts Reel	Ribbons and Hearts 2

7 Quilting Stencils (Layer 3)
Leaves

Maple Leaves

Maple Leaf Ring

Leaves

Leaf Wreath with 4 Points

Small Leaf Wreath with 4 Points

Leaf Wreath with 5 Points

Leaf Wreath with 6 Points

Leaf Wreath

Leaves and Hearts

Oak Leaf and Reel

Oak Leaves and Berries

Leaves

Leaves II

Leaf Cable

Leaf Ring

Leaf Ring 2

Leaf Square

7 Quilting Stencils (Layer 3)
Stars and Snowflakes

Stars & Beams

Star

Star II

Star-in-Square

Starburst

Stars

Rose

Flower

Flower II

Flower III

Flower IV

Snowflake

Snowflake II

Snowflake III

Snowflake IV

Tile Floor

Arabesque

Tile Overall

Tiled Stars

7 Quilting Stencils (Layer 3)
Straight and Curved Lines

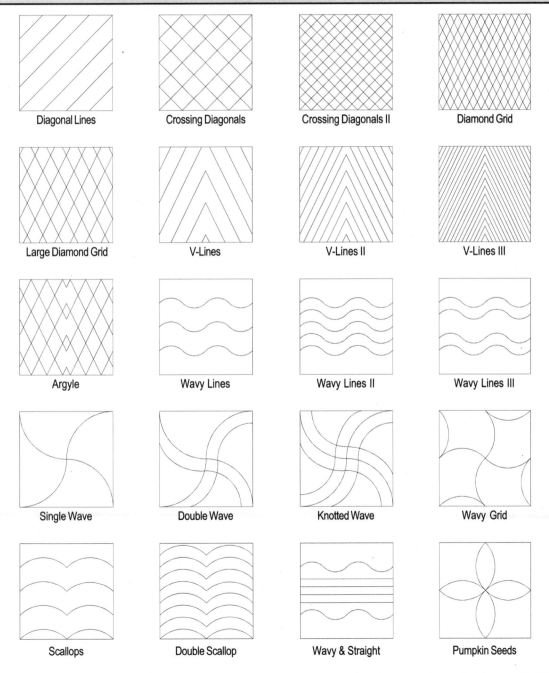

Diagonal Lines	Crossing Diagonals	Crossing Diagonals II	Diamond Grid
Large Diamond Grid	V-Lines	V-Lines II	V-Lines III
Argyle	Wavy Lines	Wavy Lines II	Wavy Lines III
Single Wave	Double Wave	Knotted Wave	Wavy Grid
Scallops	Double Scallop	Wavy & Straight	Pumpkin Seeds

Pumpkin Seeds II

Pumpkin Seeds III

Clover

Clamshell

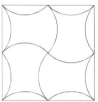

Wineglass (Straight)

Seeds & Waves

7 Quilting Stencils (Layer 3)
Wreaths

Feather Wreath with Heart

Heart Wreath

Sunflower Wreath

Heart Wreath 2

Heart Wreath 3

Petal Wreath

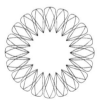

Petal Wreath 2

Sawtooth Wreath

Feather Wreath 2

Looped Ring Wreath

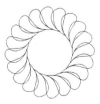

Feather Wreath 3

Feather Wreath 4

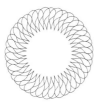

Feather Wreath 5

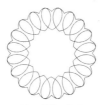

Heart Wreath 4

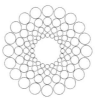

Circle Wreath

Simple Wreath

8 Overlaid Blocks

A is for Apple

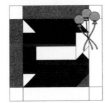

B is for Balloon

C is for Car

D is for Drum

E is for Elephant

F is for Football

G is for Guitar

H is for Horse

I is for Ice Cream Cone

J is for Jack-in-the-Box

K is for Kite

L is for Ladybug

M is for Moon

N is for Nutcracker

O is for Octopus

P is for Pig

Q is for Queen

R is for Rocket

S is for Sun

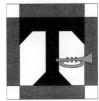

T is for Trumpet

U is for Umbrella

V is for Violin

W is for Watermelon Slice

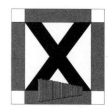
X is for Xylophone

Y is for Yarn

Z is for Zinnia

8 Overlaid Blocks
Fancy Flowers

Purple Petals

Rotate Surprise

Flowering Ohio Star

Flowering Wheel

Rising Waves

Valentine Album

Flower-in-the-Box

Fall Dance

Trellis

9-Patch Flower

Stained-Glass Window

Scattered Leaves

Blooming Orchid

Glass Sunflower

Spring Flowers

Shady Window

8 Overlaid Blocks
Pictures

Sailor's Delight

Fancy Fruit

Fall Flowers

Sunny Sail

First Bloom

Christmas Morning

Presents Under the Tree

Evening Sail

Snowy Day

Barn Friends

On the Lookout

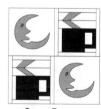
Sweet Dreams

Wake Up

A Flock

Apple Tree

Sleep Tight

8 Overlaid Blocks
Simple Designs

Fan and Stars

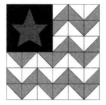

Stars and Stripes

Captured Feathers

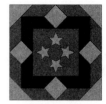

Framed Stars

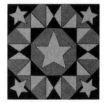

Star within Stars

Diamond Flower

Spiral Roses

Fanned Flowers

Flying Stars

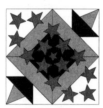

Rotating Stars

Now Showing

Spinning Snowflake

Woven Petals

Texas Wheel

Grapes of Wrath

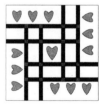

Heart Lattice

Index

Blocks beginning with Numbers